# The Thirty-Six Stratagems for Young Minds

## The Hidden Crossing

Edited by **KaDa Gushi** and **Hongyan Mao**
Illustrated by **Chen Wei Studio**

RC
Books Beyond Boundaries
ROYAL COLLINS

Wearing a flowing white robe, shining armor, and a longbow strapped to his back, the warrior raced forward on his majestic white horse, gripping a gleaming Fangtian halberd.

Who was this awe-inspiring general in white?

He was none other than Xue Rengui, the famous general of the Tang Dynasty.

In the year 645 AD, Emperor Tang Taizong led a grand military expedition against Goguryeo, appointing Zhang Shigui as the army's commander.

At that time, Xue Rengui was just a low-ranking soldier under Zhang's command, following the army into battle.

After three months of marching, the 300,000-strong army finally reached the edge of the sea.

Across the vast waters lay their enemy—Goguryeo.

Three hundred mighty warships stood ready along the shore. The soldiers, fully armed, awaited the emperor's command to set sail.

Emperor Tang Taizong had fought countless battles and won many victories, yet he had never fought at sea. This was the first time he had ever seen the ocean.

The crashing waves surged like a thousand galloping warhorses, rocking the massive warships back and forth. Even standing still became a challenge. The emperor's head spun, his vision blurred—his fear of the sea took hold.

Terrified, Emperor Taizong hurried off the ship. Turning to Zhang Shigui, he declared, “The sea is unpredictable, and who knows what monsters lurk beneath the waves? If something happens to our ships, we will all be doomed! We must find another way to cross!”

But the endless ocean stretched before them. Swimming across was impossible, and building a bridge was unthinkable.

The land route would take too long. What could they do?

The generals pleaded, "Your Majesty, our warships are strong, and our navy trains at sea daily. There is no danger!"

"No, no, no! It is too risky!" The emperor waved his hands frantically, refusing to set foot on a ship.

Zhang Shigui grew increasingly anxious. He couldn't eat or sleep, and his beard grew thinner from all the stress.

Just then, Xue Rengui approached him with an idea. “The emperor fears the sea so that he won’t board willingly. But I have a way to get him across without him realizing it.”

Early the next morning, Zhang Shigui, beaming with excitement, reported to the emperor, "Your Majesty, a wealthy merchant, has heard of your campaign against Goguryeo. He wishes to donate supplies for our army!"

Emperor Taizong clapped his hands in delight. "Excellent! Bring him to me at once!"

An elderly man with snow-white hair and a beard appeared before the emperor. Strangely, despite his age, his face had no wrinkles—it was as smooth as that of a young man.

Bowing deeply, the old man said, "Your Majesty's victory is certain! I have already stored supplies in a warehouse near the shore. Everything is ready to be loaded onto ships."

The emperor, accompanied by his generals, followed the old merchant to the warehouse. The supplies for 300,000 soldiers were stored here, covered tightly with cloth.

The merchant led Emperor Taizong into the largest chamber. Inside, silk curtains hung from the ceiling, creating a luxurious palace-like atmosphere. The thick carpets underfoot felt soft and comforting.

A feast was laid out on a grand table. The merchant invited the emperor and his generals to sit, pouring wine for them.

As the music played and wine flowed, the emperor and his generals celebrated for days, enjoying the lavish hospitality.

One evening, as the emperor and his men drank, the table suddenly began to shake. Plates and cups crashed to the floor, and the silk curtains billowed wildly as if caught in a storm. From outside, a deafening roar echoed—like thunderous waves crashing.

At first, Emperor Taizong thought he had simply had too much to drink. But something felt wrong.

“Pull back the curtains!” he ordered.

The moment the curtains were drawn, he gasped in shock.

Beyond the silk drapes, endless ocean waves stretched as far as the eye could see. Towering swells crashed and roared around them.

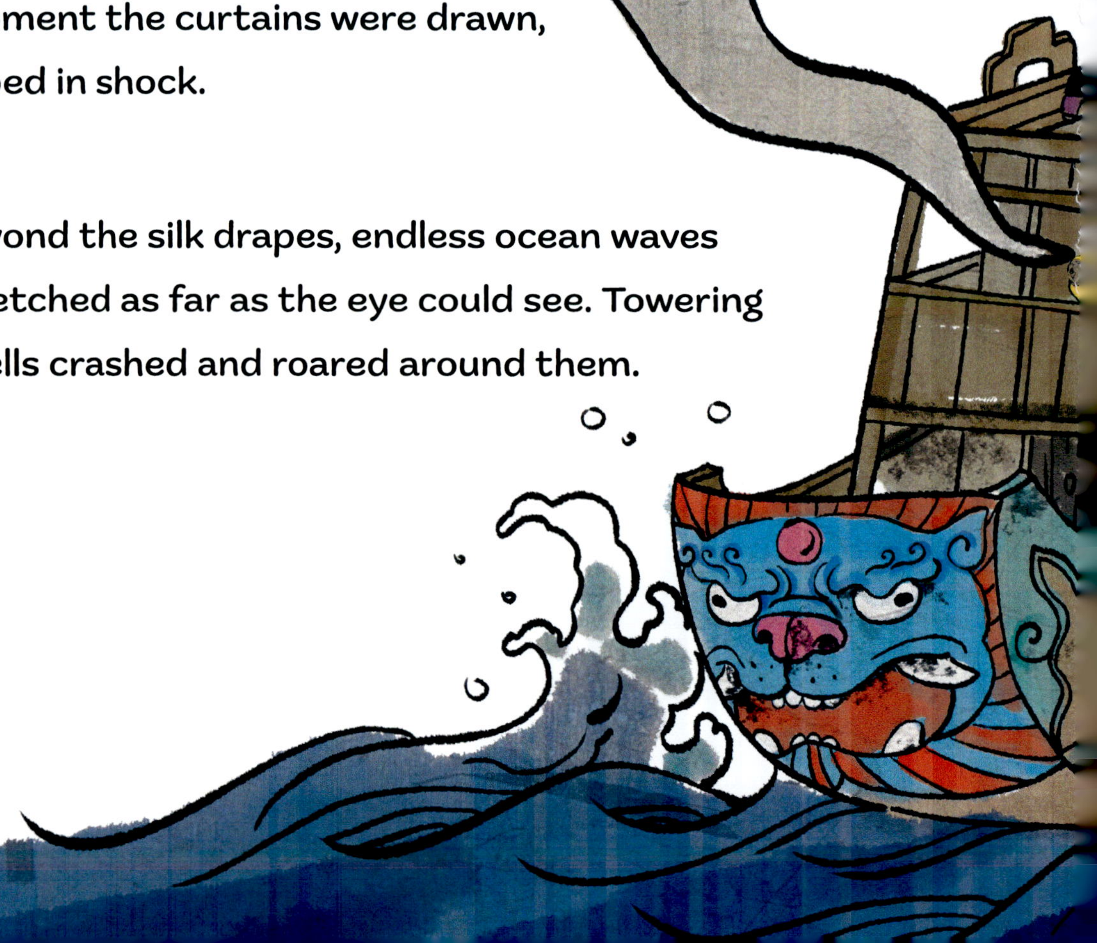

This was no luxurious chamber—it was the deck of a massive warship!

Panicked, the emperor shouted, "Where are we?!"

Zhang Shigui stepped forward and bowed. "Your Majesty, we are already sailing across the sea. With the wind at our backs, we will soon reach Goguryeo."

The old merchant also fell to his knees, pleading, "Forgive us, Your Majesty! We had to trick you to get across the sea safely."

Then, the merchant removed his white wig and beard. It was Xue Rengui!

The emperor stared in shock. Then, seeing that they had crossed safely and his dignity remained intact, he burst into laughter.

"Well done! What a brilliant strategy!" he praised.

Thus, Xue Rengui used clever deception to help the emperor overcome his fear and cross the sea without realizing it. Since emperors were called the "Son of Heaven," this tactic of using illusion and misdirection was later known as "Hiding the Sky and Crossing the Sea."

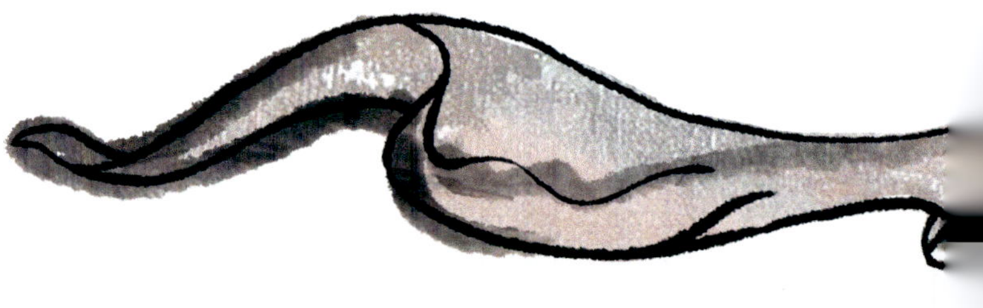

On the battlefield in Goguryeo, Xue Rengui, clad in white robes, fought with unmatched courage.

Emperor Taizong declared, “Winning in Liaodong is not my greatest joy. My greatest victory is discovering Xue Rengui, the White-Robed General!”

From that day forward, Xue Rengui was honored as one of the greatest generals in Tang history.

# Historical Notes

## Emperor Taizong (Li Shimin)

The second emperor of the Tang Dynasty was known for his wise governance and military prowess. He reformed the imperial examination system, promoted agriculture, and reduced tax burdens on the people, ushering in the Golden Age of the Tang Dynasty.

## Xue Rengui

A legendary Tang general who joined the army at age 30. His three consecutive arrow strikes in battle became famous, earning him the nickname:

*"The General Whose Three Arrows Conquered the Heavens."*

## Zhang Shigui

He was a trusted general of Tang Taizong, renowned for his immense strength and unwavering loyalty. He was appointed commander of the Imperial Guards, responsible for protecting the emperor.

## Moral of the Story

Courage is not the absence of fear but the ability to overcome it—sometimes with a little clever thinking!

### Fangtian Halberd

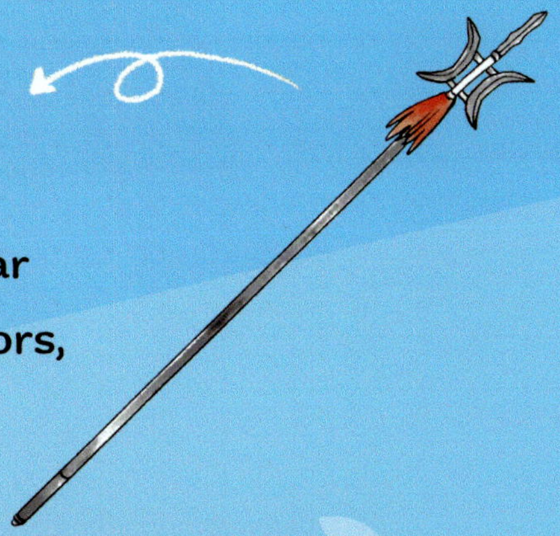

A powerful weapon that combined a spear and axe-like blade. Used by famous warriors, including Lü Bu of the Three Kingdoms.

### Tang Dynasty Warships

The Tang army's largest warships were three-story battle vessels carrying up to 800 soldiers and equipped with advanced naval weaponry.

### Tiger-Head Helmets

During the Tang Dynasty, tiger-head helmets were popular among warriors. Designed with large round eyes and fierce expressions, these helmets made generals look even more imposing. Archaeological excavations at the tomb of General Yuchi Jingde have uncovered vividly painted warrior figurines wearing tiger-head helmets.

# About the Editor

**Mao Hongyan** is the associate editor of *Happy Chinese Language and Composition*, a children's magazine. With a deep passion for children's literature, she is highly dedicated to children's growth and has extensive experience in children's book planning. She understands child psychology and cognitive development, crafting texts that align with young readers' psychological characteristics. Her works are beloved by children and parents alike. She has published *Interactive Sound Book: Fun with Chinese Idioms*, produced by Lelequ.

# About the Illustrator

**Chen Wei**, born in 1979 in Taizhou, Jiangsu, graduated from the Design Department of Xi'an Academy of Fine Arts.

His notable picture books include *A New Resident in Kano Town*, *The Mice of Rose Villa*, and *The Frog and the Boy*. Among them, *The Frog and the Boy* won the Second Feng Zikai Children's Picture Book Award Jury Prize. His works have been translated and published in Taiwan, Hong Kong, and South Korea.

The Thirty-Six Stratagems for Young Minds: The Hidden Crossing

Edited by KaDa Gushi and Hongyan Mao
Illustrated by Chen Wei Studio

First published in 2025 by Royal Collins Publishing Group Inc.
Groupe Publication Royal Collins Inc.
550-555 boul. René-Lévesque O Montréal (Québec) H2Z1B1 Canada



ISBN: 978-1-4878-1336-9

To find out more about our publications,
please visit www.royalcollins.com.